AIRPLANES IN THE GARDEN

Monarch Butterflies Take Flight

Joan Z. Calder
Illustrated by Cathy Quiel

KAWARTHA LAKES

PATIO
PUBLISHING

Santa Barbara, California

ACKNOWLEDGMENTS

John Calder   June Scharenbroch Gail Esola

Penelope C. Paine Rose Nevarez Isaac Hernández

The monarch caterpillars that rode home in my truck

Bonnie, Sergio, Stanley – students at UCSB

Dr. Karen S. Oberhauser, University of Minnesota

Dr. Robert Michael Pyle, the Xerces Society Nick de Pencier

Dr. Orley R. "Chip" Taylor, Director of Monarch Watch

PATIO PUBLISHING

Patio Publishing, 302 Santa Anita Road, Santa Barbara, CA 93105 • info@patiopublishing.com

Publisher's Cataloging-in-Publication

Calder, Joan Z. (Joan Zipperer)
    Airplanes in the garden : monarch butterflies take
flight / Joan Z. Calder ; illustrated by Cathy Quiel. --
1st ed.
    p. cm.
    SUMMARY: An imaginative young girl learns about the wonders of nature and the secrets of metamorphosis as she observes two special caterpillars--from the moment she discovers their eggs on the milkweed leaves in her garden until their emergence as beautiful monarch butterflies. Also includes tips on growing a butterfly-friendly garden, maps of the monarch migration, and a butterfly song.
    Audience: Ages 4-8.
    ISBN-13: 978-0-9832962-1-8
    ISBN-10: 0-9832962-1-9
    LCCN2011923677

1. Monarch butterfly--Juvenile literature.
    2. Monarch butterfly--Life cycles--Juvenile literature.
    [1. Monarch butterfly. 2. Butterflies. 3. Metamorphosis.]
    I. Quiel, Cathy, ill. II. Title.

QL544.2.C35 2011   595.78'9
                QBI11-600079

The artwork was created with watercolor
The text is set in 17-point Monotype Fournier
Book design by Isaac Hernández/IsaacHernandez.com

To contact author, visit www.airplanesinthegarden.com
To contact illustrator, visit www.cathyquiel.com
To contact songwriter, visit www.reverbnation.com/rebeccatroon

First Edition 10 9 8 7 6 5 4 3

Printed with soy-based ink in the United States of America by Worzalla, Stevens Point, WI

To
John
Alexander
Aubrey
Gretchen
Brian
Thank you for chasing
butterflies with me.
— JZC

To my husband John and sons Ryan and Tyler,
for giving me a life of love and for joining me
in the world of imagination. To my parents who
didn't blink an eye when I wanted to major in art.
— CQ

Bonnie smiled as she sniffed the perfume of the sweet peas. Tall grasses waved and whispered in the breeze. Of all the things in the family garden, she loved the orange and black monarch butterflies the best.

"What are you
watching?" Bonnie's
mom asked, as she
walked toward the flowers.

"Mom, there are airplanes in the
garden!" Bonnie said.

"There are what?" her mom replied,
surprised, looking up at the sky.

6

"Airplanes! I make believe the butterflies are airplanes and the flowers are airports," Bonnie said. "The butterfly airplanes pick up babies and moms and dads to take them on a trip, and ladybug flight attendants serve cheese sandwiches to the passengers."

"What an imagination!" her mom said, smiling, and she gave Bonnie a hug.

"Do you know butterflies land on blossoms to drink
nectar with their long tongues?" Bonnie's mom asked.

"Oh, that's like when I use a straw to drink milk," Bonnie said.

"Yes, and look at this, Bonnie," her mom said, pointing to a white dot on the underside of a milkweed leaf. "A mama monarch laid this egg. It will take about thirty days for the egg to change into a butterfly. First the egg will hatch, then it will grow into a white, black, and yellow striped caterpillar that looks like a little tiger with black wiggly tentacles on both ends."

"How funny!" Bonnie giggled.

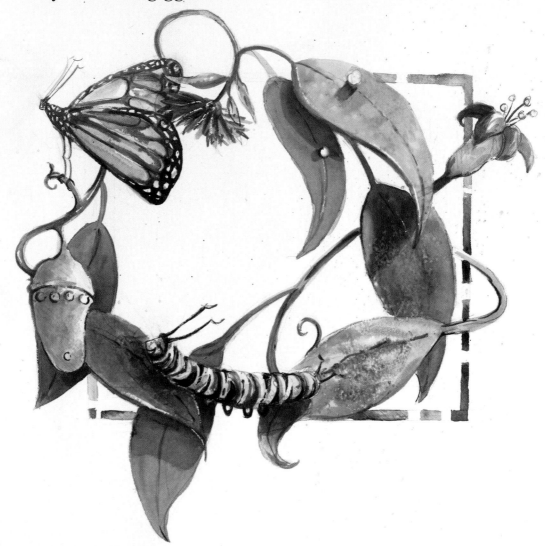

"And finally the caterpillar will turn into a beautiful orange and black butterfly," her mom explained. "The changing from an egg, to a caterpillar, to a chrysalis, to a butterfly is called complete metamorphosis.

"Met a MORRR fa *what*?" tried Bonnie. Then she looked at the milkweed plant and said, "I'm going to call this 'the-plant-that-grows-butterflies.'"

Each day, Bonnie checked to see
if the egg had turned into a caterpillar yet. Four days
later, she saw something move on the-plant-that-grows-butterflies.

Bonnie called, "Mom, Dad, look what I found!"

Bonnie's mom and dad hurried to find her in the garden, her nose
almost touching the milkweed. A caterpillar, so small she could barely
see it, wriggled on the leaf.

Then she found another. And another. Lots of tiny caterpillars covered the-plant-that-grows-butterflies.

"Hmm," Bonnie said excitedly, "I guess we will have lots of airplanes in our garden."

For ten days Bonnie watched her two favorite caterpillars grow bigger and bigger. "You are Sergio," she named the one with one short tentacle. "And you are Stanley," she said, grinning at the larger caterpillar as he climbed up a leaf.

Sergio and Stanley mowed down the edges of milkweed leaves the way Bonnie ate corn on the cob, row after row. They ate so much that soon only a few ragged leaves were left on the plant.

MONARCH

MILK
WEED

The next morning when Bonnie went to check on Sergio and Stanley, she did not find them on the-plant-that-grows-butterflies. She did not find them near her favorite rock or under the sweet peas. She searched under the big yellow flowers. No Sergio. No Stanley.

"Mom! Dad! Sergio and Stanley have disappeared!" she said sadly. "I can't find them anywhere."

All day Bonnie wondered where Stanley and Sergio had gone. She sat near the mostly eaten milkweed and wiped a tear from her cheek. Then she looked down and saw a caterpillar making its way up the steps.

"Stanley, is that you? Please be careful! If you walk on the steps, you might get SMUUUSHED." She put her hand beside him, and Stanley crawled up. Bonnie laughed when she felt Stanley's six legs tickle her hand.

"Thank you for being here. I love you."

Bonnie put her hand next to the-plant-that-grows-butterflies, and Stanley walked onto the leaf. "Stanley, you move so fast, you must be training for your takeoffs and landings. Soon you'll have wings and be able to fly!"

Seventeen days after finding the monarch eggs, Bonnie saw a caterpillar hanging upside-down from the flowerpot outside her bedroom window.

"Wow, this must be Stanley! He looks like the letter J," Bonnie told her mom and dad. "He came back to be close to me."

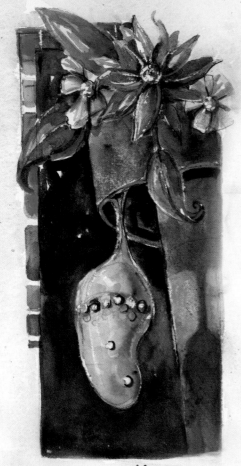

By the next day Bonnie
and her dad were looking at
a new Stanley. "Stanley turned
into a chrysalis," her dad said.
He had turned from a J into
a green bundle with dots of
glistening gold. "He is inside
the chrysalis rearranging
himself to become a butterfly."

Is Sergio somewhere
rearranging himself, too?
Bonnie thought.

Bonnie spent hours in front
of the flowerpot, watching
the bright green of the brand
new chrysalis turn into a
beautiful blue-green gem
eight days later.

She could hardly wait.

It had been almost thirty days since her mom showed her the eggs on the milkweed. Now she could see the orange and black butterfly wings through the shell of the chrysalis.

How could a butterfly's wings be stuffed into such a small space? Bonnie wondered.

As she sat alone watching, something was happening inside the precious bundle. It seemed to be pulsing like a heartbeat.

Then a crack appeared.

Suddenly Bonnie
yelled, "Mom! Dad!
Stanley broke through
the chrysalis and
is trying to get out."

Her mom and dad arrived to see
the newborn butterfly, all scrunched up,
clinging to the tattered shell.

Bonnie was worried. "Mom, what's
wrong with Stanley?"

"Oh, Bonnie, he's all right. Stanley is
pumping blood through his wings so they
become wide and flat and strong,
and then he can fly," her mom said.

As Stanley was drying off, his wings made small, silent, flapping movements. "Oh, Stanley — you're sooooo beautiful!" Bonnie cooed.

Then, after a long, long time in the warm sunshine, Stanley took his first flight. "Go Stanley, go!" Bonnie cheered, and chased after him.

Soon, another monarch was flying next to Stanley. The two butterflies flew in circles around Bonnie. "Sergio, Sergio! You came back to be with your friends, Stanley and me!"

Then Sergio and Stanley tested their landing skills on a group of zinnias and sampled the nectar. Bonnie looked up, amazed at the flutter of orange and black wings flying toward her.

Bonnie smiled up at the cloud of flapping wings. "Now we have lots and lots of beautiful airplanes in my garden."

FALL MIGRATION

Monarchs west of the Rocky Mountains travel to small groves of trees along the California coast. Those east of the Rocky Mountains fly farther south, perhaps 1200–2500 miles (1900–4000 km) to the forests high in the mountains of Mexico. Some monarchs live in Florida and Texas during winter.

The monarch migration is driven by seasonal changes. Day length and temperature changes influence the movement of the monarchs.

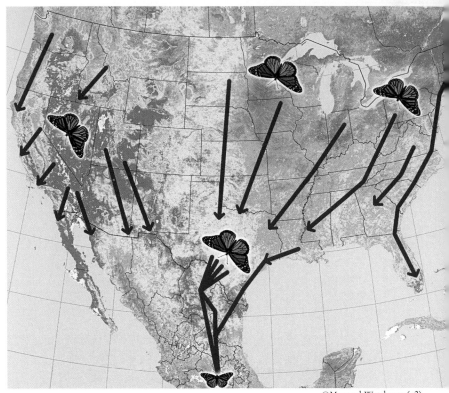

©MonarchWatch.org (x2)

SPRING-SUMMER MIGRATION

The same butterflies that made the journey south in the fall will begin their return trip in March. The migrants fly to the southern U.S. where they mate and lay eggs.

Their descendants will continue the migration north. By the time the monarchs arrive at the border of Canada and the U.S., they may be the great-grandchildren of the original butterflies that left the previous spring.

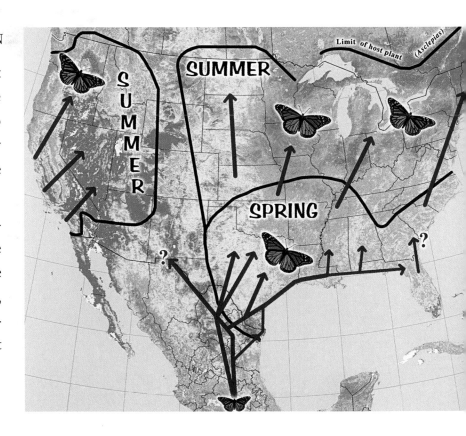

For more information on monarch migrations visit www.monarchwatch.org.

Learn about Stanley and Sergio

🦋 Butterflies are pollinators.

🦋 The long tongue used to drink nectar is called a proboscis (pro·bos·cis). A butterfly must assemble its proboscis as soon as it emerges from the chrysalis (KRIS·uh·lis).

🦋 Transforming from an egg to a butterfly is called complete metamorphosis (met·uh·MAWR·fuh·sis).

🦋 Butterflies taste with their feet. Taste receptors on a butterfly's feet help it find its host plant and locate food.

🦋 The fleshy "antennas" on each end of the monarch caterpillar are not actually antennae, but sense organs. They are called filaments or tentacles.

🦋 Males have a black spot on a vein on each hind wing. Females have thicker vein lines and no black spot on their hind wings.

🦋 Monarchs can fly if the temperature is above 60°F (16°C), and above 50°F (10°C), if it is sunny. The sun warms their flight muscles enough so they can fly.

🦋 A butterfly will occasionally sip from mud puddles which are rich in minerals and salts. This behavior is called puddling.

🦋 Butterflies breathe through spiracles, tiny air tubes on the sides of their bodies that carry air from the outside directly to body tissues.

Visit www.airplanesinthegarden.com to learn more

Female monarch butterfly

Male monarch butterfly

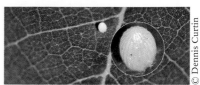
© Dennis Curtin
Egg under milkweed leave

© Larry Scheunemann
Caterpillar

© Kristin Fonseca
Caterpillar forming a J

© Harry Hooper
Early-stage chrysalis

© Joanna S. Billings
Monarch about to break the chrysalis

© Kristin Fonseca
Monarch drying new wings

© Marilyn Wockley
Monarch feeding on nectar

© MonarchWatch.org (x2)

PLANT A GARDEN TO HELP FRIENDS OF STANLEY AND SERGIO

The monarch migration is truly one of the world's greatest natural wonders, yet it is threatened by habitat loss in North America—at the overwintering sites and throughout the spring and summer breeding range as well. You can create a paradise for butterflies by planting a garden of caterpillar host plants and nectar plants, and you will be contributing to monarch conservation.

- Monarch butterflies require two types of foods.

    The caterpillar stage requires milkweed—caterpillars eat the leaves. The botanical name for milkweed is Asclepias (Üh-SKLEE-pea-us).

    The butterfly stage requires nectar—butterflies drink nectar with their proboscis.

- Choose a location in full sun.

    Monarchs require warmth to fly. Plants require sunlight to blossom.

- Herbicides and pesticides kill butterflies. Learn safe alternatives.

- Plant the milkweed where it will not be disturbed.

    The caterpillars like to wander to find the best place to make their chrysalis.

- Plant milkweed in groups of two to four plants around the garden.

- Choose flowering shrubs native to your area to provide nectar. Check with your local nursery for suggestions of host and nectar plants that attract butterflies.

- Plant nectar plants near the milkweed. Select flowers that bloom at different times so your garden provides nectar from spring through autumn. Butterflies typically visit flowers that are bright and provide landing platforms.

- Nectar plants:

Aster	Marigold	Lantana
Zinnia	Bee Balm	Mexican Sunflower
Cosmos	Verbena	Black-eyed Susan
Goldenrod	Joe-Pye Weed	Wild Bergamot

- Provide a water source. Butterflies like wet sand or mud to get minerals.

- Locate a seating area nearby to watch your new friends.

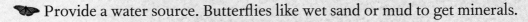

For more information on preserving monarch habitat, please visit: www.monarchwatch.org/waystations/

FLY AWAY

by Rebecca Troon

A larvae crawls from a tiny egg
Munches milkweed leaves all day
She grows and grows, then sheds her skin
Her colors warn of poison within.

    Oh, fly away
    Fly we say
    Everybody fly one day
    The caterpillar can only crawl
    But the butterfly flies away.

She stores her fat for a special day
Then forms herself in the shape of a "J"
Sheds to reveal a chrysalis
It's time for her metamorphosis.

Tick tock, tick tock, twelve days pass
The butterfly comes out at last
She dries her wings, rests in a gum tree
Sips flower nectar oh so sweet.

She travels on for many days
Finds a mate and lays her eggs
Orange, black and white she flashes by
The lovely monarch butterfly.

KAWARTHA LAKES

To hear and download "Fly Away," sung by Rebecca,
please visit www.reverbnation.com/rebeccatroon